Good Character Traits

Dependability

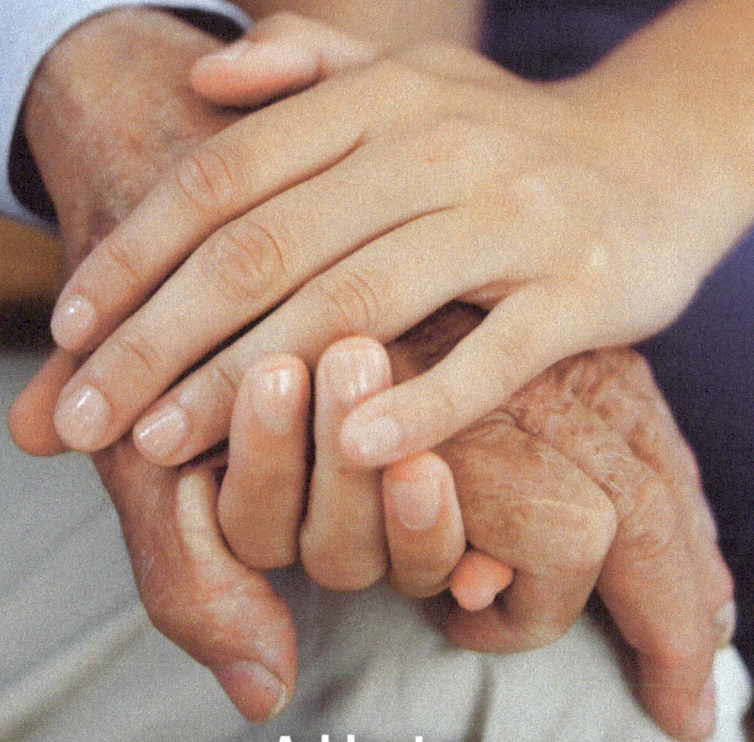

Ashley Lee

Explore other books at:
WWW.ENGAGEBOOKS.COM

VANCOUVER, B.C.

e WWW.ENGAGEBOOKS.COM

Dependability: Good Character Traits
Lee, Ashley, 1995 –
Text © 2025 Engage Books
Design © 2025 Engage Books

Edited by: A.R. Roumanis
Design by: Mandy Christiansen

Text set in Myriad Pro Regular.
Chapter headings set in Anton.

FIRST EDITION / FIRST PRINTING

LIBRARY AND ARCHIVES CANADA CATALOGUING IN PUBLICATION

Title: Dependability / Ashley Lee.
Names: Lee, Ashley, author.
Description: Series statement: Good Character Traits

ISBN 978-1-77878-736-2 (hardcover)
ISBN 978-1-77878-742-3 (softcover)

This project has been made possible in part by the Government of Canada.

Canadä

Dependability

Contents

What Is Dependability?

Dependability means doing what you say you will do. It means other people can count on you.

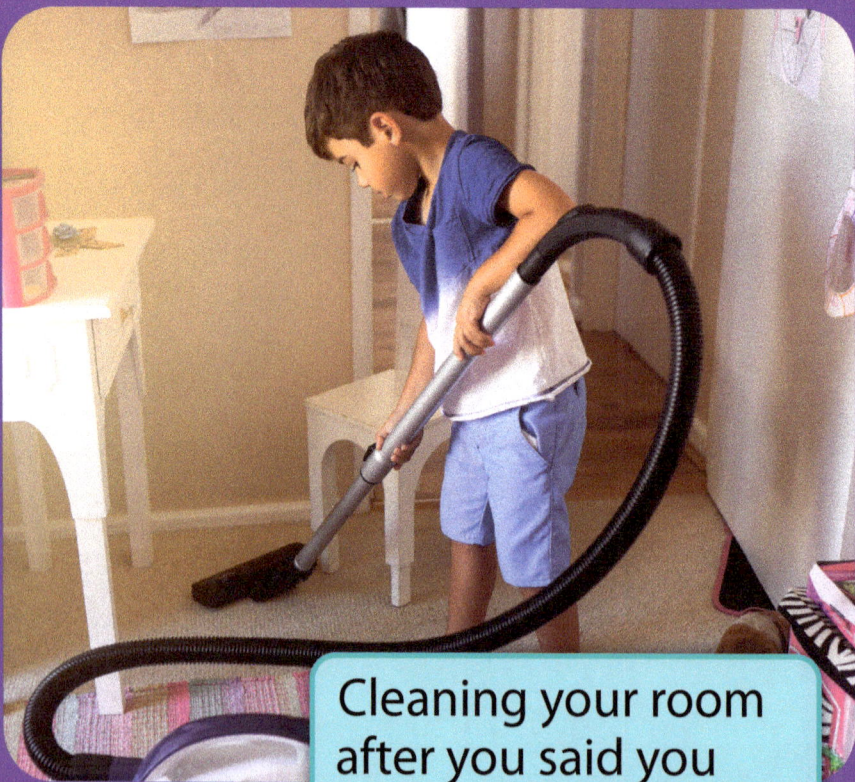

Cleaning your room after you said you would is dependable.

It also means you help out when needed. You also own up to your mistakes and say sorry when you hurt someone.

Why Is Dependability Important?

Dependability helps things run smoothly. Your teacher depends on you to show up to school on time so they do not have to explain things again.

Dependability also helps people **trust** each other. Trust helps people become better friends.

Key Word

Trust: the feeling that someone is there for you and believes in you.

What Does Dependability Look Like?

People who are dependable are not late. They make sure to finish their work and chores on time.

Dependable people keep their **promises**. They do not forget about the things they said they would do.

Key Word

Promises: when someone says they definitely will or will not do something.

How Does Dependability Affect You?

Being dependable helps you grow as a person. It helps you build **confidence**. Confidence makes you want to try new things.

Key Word

Confidence: the feeling of believing in yourself.

Being dependable can make you feel happier. It feels good to keep your promises and not have to worry about them.

How Does Dependability Affect Others?

Being dependable can make others feel **valued**. They feel like you care about them and their time.

Being dependable can also make other people less **stressed**. They do not have to worry about something getting done if you are dependable.

Key Word

Stressed: when people feel uncomfortable about something that is happening.

Is Everyone Dependable?

Not everyone is dependable. Some people are not dependable on purpose. Others may have problems remembering things.

But everyone can become dependable by practicing. Practicing means doing something over and over again to get better at it.

Is It Bad if You Are Not Dependable?

It is not bad if you are not dependable. But it can cause problems for you. Friends may stop trusting you.

It is important to say sorry if you forget to do something on time. Tell the person you let down that you will try harder next time.

Does Dependability Change Over Time?

Some people become more dependable as they get older. They learn how important it is and have lots of practice.

Mental health problems can make a dependable person less dependable. Getting help can make them more dependable again.

Key Word

Mental health: the health of your mind.

Is It Hard to Be Dependable?

It can be hard to be dependable if you want to do something else. You may have homework to do but want to play with your friends instead.

It can also be hard to be dependable when you have a lot to do. This can make you feel stressed or like you do not want to do anything.

Ask for help if you feel like you have too many things to do.

How Can You Learn to Be More Dependable?

Keep a journal of the things you need to do or said you would do. This will help you remember to do them all.

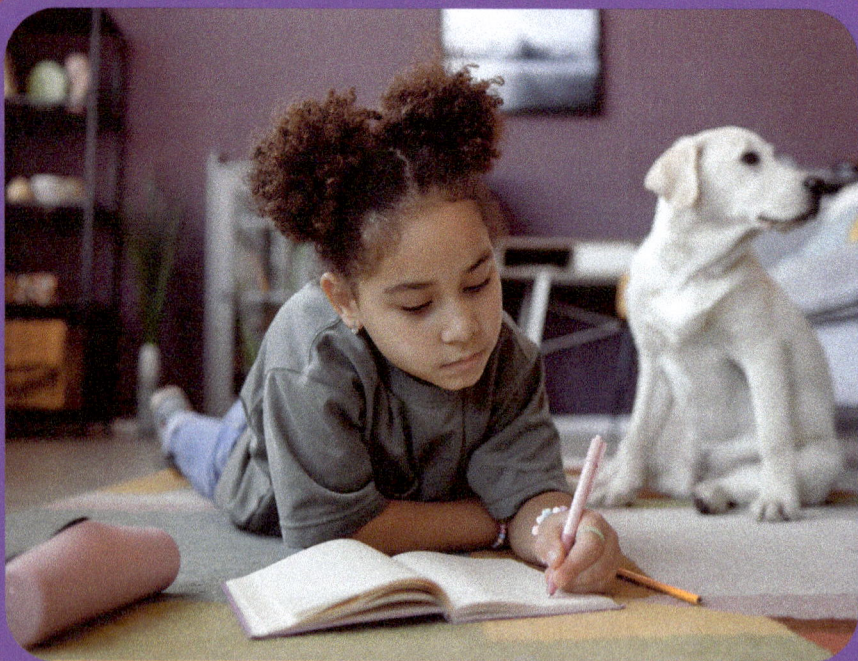

Create a **routine** for things you do a lot. You are less likely to forget to do something if you do it at the same time every day.

Key Word

Routine: doing the same things at the same time each day.

How Can You Help Others Be More Dependable?

Talk openly about why it is important to be dependable. Tell others how it makes you feel when they are not dependable.

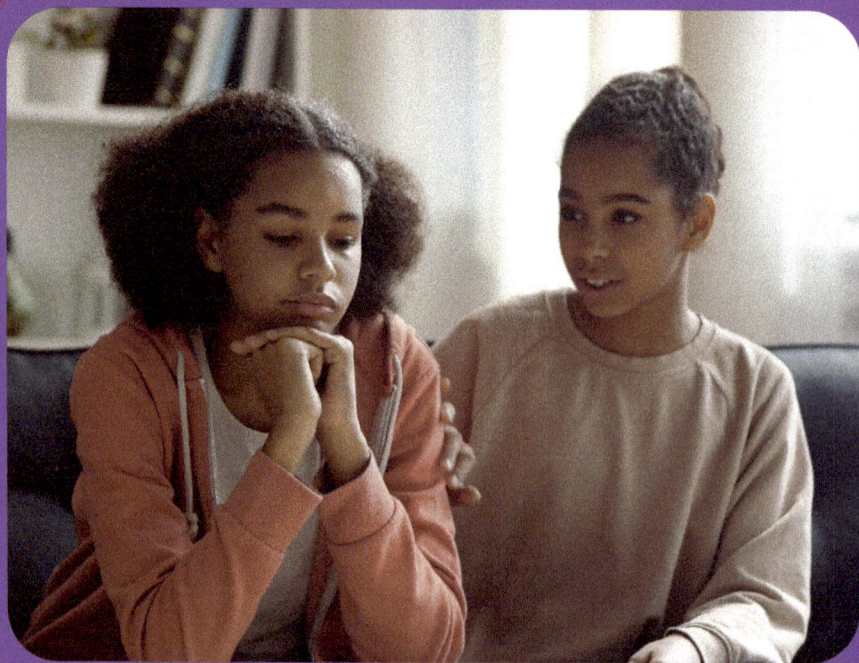

Let others know how **proud** you are when they are dependable. Be understanding when they have a hard time with dependability.

Key Word

Proud: feeling good because of something you or someone else has done

How to Be Dependable Every Day

1. Give yourself lots of time to get ready and do homework.

2. Set a timer when getting ready so you will not be late.

3. Tell someone right away if you cannot keep plans with them.

4. Do not make promises you know you cannot keep.

Dependability Around the World

Lots of fruits and vegetables need warm weather to grow. But many countries are cold for all or part of the year.

Warmer countries send fruits and vegetables to colder countries. These colder countries depend on the warmer ones to get them their food quickly.

People depend on these fruits and vegetables to stay healthy.

Quiz

Test your knowledge of dependability by answering the following questions. The questions are based on what you have read in this book. The answers are listed on the bottom of the next page.

1 Does dependability mean you help out when needed?

2 Do dependable people keep their promises?

3 Can being dependable make others feel valued?

4 How can everyone become dependable?

5 What should you do if you feel like you have too many things to do?

6 Should you make promises you know you cannot keep?

Explore Other Level 2 Readers.

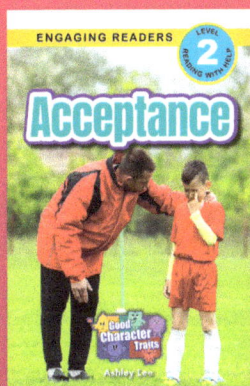

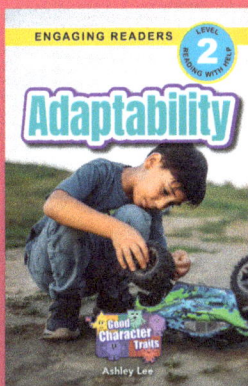

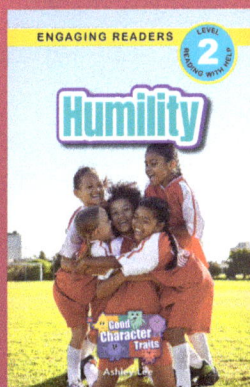

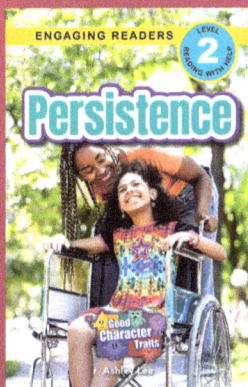

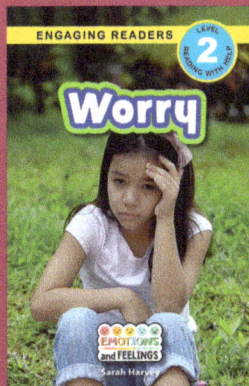

ENGAGING READERS — LEVEL 2 — READING WITH HELP

Acceptance — Good Character Traits — Ashley Lee

Adaptability — Good Character Traits — Ashley Lee

Forgiveness — Good Character Traits — Ashley Lee

Humility — Good Character Traits — Ashley Lee

Persistence — Good Character Traits — Ashley Lee

Gratitude — Emotions and Feelings — Sarah Harvey

Grief — Emotions and Feelings — Sarah Harvey

Love — Emotions and Feelings — Sarah Harvey

Worry — Emotions and Feelings — Sarah Harvey

Visit www.engagebooks.com/readers

www.ingramcontent.com/pod-product-compliance
Lightning Source LLC
Chambersburg PA
CBHW052035030426
42337CB00027B/5015